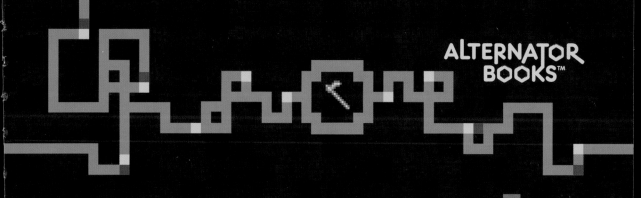

ALTERNATOR BOOKS™

THE
UNOFFICIAL
GUIDE
TO
MINECRAFT
MINING AND FARMING

HEATHER E. SCHWARTZ

Lerner Publications ◆ Minneapolis

BIG THANKS TO CONNOR KNIGHT AND NOLAN SCHWARTZ FOR CREATING THE PICTURES FOR THIS BOOK. YOU ROCK!

Lerner Publications Company
A division of Lerner Publishing Group, Inc.
241 First Avenue North
Minneapolis, MN 55401 USA

For reading levels and more information, look up this title at www.lernerbooks.com.

Main body text set in Aptifer Slab LT Pro 11.5/18.
Typeface provided by Linotype AG.

Library of Congress Cataloging-in-Publication Data

Names: Schwartz, Heather E., author.
Title: The unofficial guide to Minecraft mining and farming / Heather E. Schwartz.
Description: Minneapolis : Lerner Publications, 2019. | Series: My Minecraft (Alternator Books) | Includes bibliographical references and index. | Audience: Age 7–11. | Audience: Grade 4 to 6.
Identifiers: LCCN 2018022628 (print) | LCCN 2018023486 (ebook) | ISBN 9781541543522 (eb pdf) | ISBN 9781541538856 (lb : alk. paper) | ISBN 9781541546110 (pb : alk. paper)
Subjects: LCSH: Minecraft (Game)—Juvenile literature.
Classification: LCC GV1469.M55 (ebook) | LCC GV1469.M55 S35 2019 (print) | DDC 794.8—dc23

LC record available at https://lccn.loc.gov/2018022628

Manufactured in the United States of America
1-45068-35895-8/28/2018

CONTENTS

STAYING ALIVE

YOU'RE PLAYING *MINECRAFT* IN SURVIVAL MODE. You know you've got to work to stay alive. The **livestock** and **crops** on your farm are thriving, so you won't go hungry. Soon you'll be eating meat and harvesting wheat. But there's an area of your farm you've kept dark to grow mushrooms. **Mobs** spawn, or appear, in dark places. Your farm could become dangerous if it attracts these creatures.

You decide to craft some weapons to fight off hostile mobs. You know you'll need strong armor too. Your **inventory** is low, but you have the materials for a stone pickax and a furnace. With these tools, you can mine for iron.

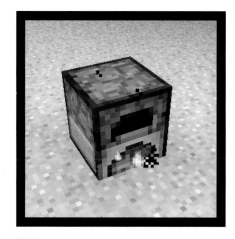

A furnace can melt down iron to make tools and weapons.

Mining for materials takes lots of planning and preparation.

Armed with plenty of torches to light your way—and ward off mobs—you head into a cave. After mining iron blocks with your pickax, you use your furnace to **smelt** the blocks into pieces you can use to make tools and weapons.

Surviving in *Minecraft* takes work. You have to be a farmer, a miner, and a fighter. But you're willing to do whatever it takes to stay in the game.

Hostile mobs will attack if you get too close.

CHAPTER 1
MAKING YOUR WAY IN
MINECRAFT

WHAT IS *MINECRAFT* ALL ABOUT? One answer is right in the name of the game. Mining and crafting are huge parts of what you do when you play. When you mine, you look for **ores** you can use to craft items such as mining and farming tools. You can also craft armor and weapons. Without them, you can't defend yourself against hostile mobs.

A *Minecraft* cave

Many kinds of ores are in *Minecraft*. You can search and dig for these ores in caves, caverns, or **ravines** in the landscape. Or you can dig your own mines. Some ores are much easier to mine than others. The ones that are difficult to mine are often more valuable. All ores are useful, though some are better than others. Coal, which is used for torches, is easy to find. So is iron. It is used to make tools, armor, and weapons. Diamonds are hard to find. They are more valuable than coal or iron. You can use them to make even stronger tools, armor, and weapons.

You can create a structure like this to help you remember what all the different kinds of ores look like while you are mining.

Farming is also important in *Minecraft*. Why? Because just like a real person, your *Minecraft* character needs food to live! You can farm all kinds of crops, including vegetables you can pick and wheat for baking bread and feeding animals. You can also farm chickens, sheep, cows, and pigs—just as you would on a real-life farm. Then you can combine ingredients from your farm to make foods such as rabbit stew or pumpkin pie.

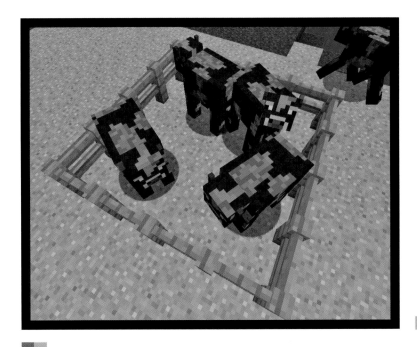

In addition to providing food, cows can also be used to make leather for armor.

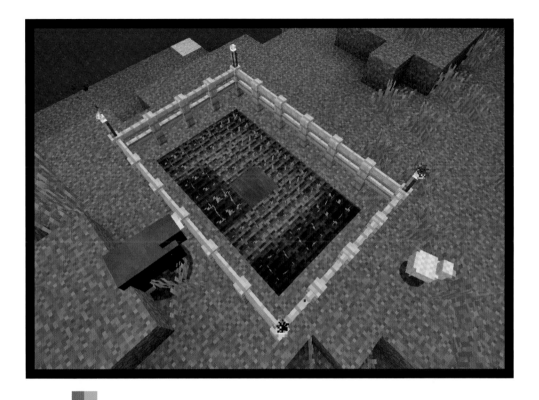

Torches can be placed around crops to give off light and help the plants grow.

To get started, you have to build a farm that will allow your crops and animals to grow and thrive. That takes grass, dirt, seeds, and a water source. You can build your farm outside, inside, or even underground. But no matter where it is, your farm needs plenty of light so your crops will grow.

How do you light an underground farm? That's where crafting comes in. You can use coal ore to create torches and place them near your crops. You can also use materials you've mined to craft tools for farming. If you have a supply of iron ore in your inventory, you'll be able to craft a garden hoe to weed your gardens and move dirt, shears to gather wool from sheep, and buckets to haul water. These are all tools you'll need for your farm to succeed.

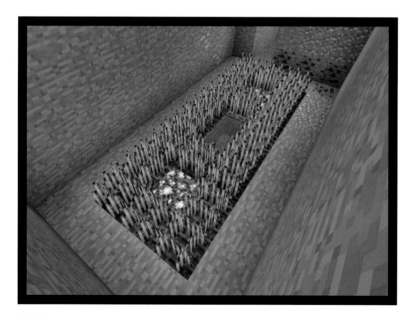

Growing crops underground is possible with lots of light.

CHAPTER 2

STAYING SAFE

IN THE WORLD OF *MINECRAFT*, BOTH MINING AND FARMING CAN PUT YOU DIRECTLY IN THE PATH OF DANGER. You could become trapped underground or run into mobs. You have to plan and be careful to stay safe.

Building a staircase is a smart way to make sure you have a quick escape route while you are mining.

When mining, you need to dig carefully. If you're digging a staircase mine, you'll want to create steps as you go so that you can climb back up to get out of the mine. If you dig more than one block down at a time, you could find yourself trapped in the very hole you've created.

Another way you could get trapped is by digging straight up or down. Either option could cause your tunnel to collapse. If you're digging down, you might fall into a deep hole. If you're digging up, gravel and sand could bury you. You'll be much safer if you don't mine the block you're standing on or the block directly over your head.

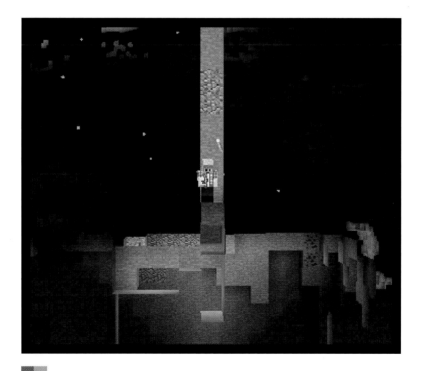

If you dig straight down, you increase the risk of falling into a cavern or a pool of lava.

STEMCRAFT

When you dig a mine in *Minecraft*, you're acting like a mining engineer. In real life, mining engineers make sure mines are safe for workers, who dig for ore deep within Earth. They help design mines so the structures won't collapse. They also develop systems for removing ores quickly and efficiently, without damaging the environment.

Large machines such as this one are used to mine ores in real life.

Be alert for liquid while you're mining. If you hit lava or water while you're digging, your character may not survive. Listen for dripping sounds that could be a sign you're about to hit water or lava.

Watch out for mobs as you mine dark caves!

As careful as you may be, you could still encounter another danger: hostile mobs. Mobs are often in dark places such as caves, so be sure to light your way with torches and carry plenty of weapons to fight them off.

Lava flowing out into a mine

Mobs can also show up near your farm. Some crops, like mushrooms, grow best in the dark. But if you don't light up the area, you may attract mobs. So you should design a growing space where mobs can't spawn. You'll have to place torches strategically, so they keep mobs away but don't provide too much light for the mushrooms.

This mushroom patch has just enough light to keep mobs away while the mushrooms grow.

CHAPTER 3

UPPING YOUR GAME

READY FOR A *MINECRAFT* CHALLENGE?
Try mining for diamonds. They're rare, so they're hard to find, but diamonds are the best material for making tools, weapons, and armor.

To mine for diamonds, you need good, strong mining tools and equipment. An iron pickax is used for digging your mine, and an iron sword and iron shield can help you defend against mobs. Next, you need to know where to look. Diamonds are in deep layers of the *Minecraft* world. But even if you reach these layers, diamond ore can be difficult to find.

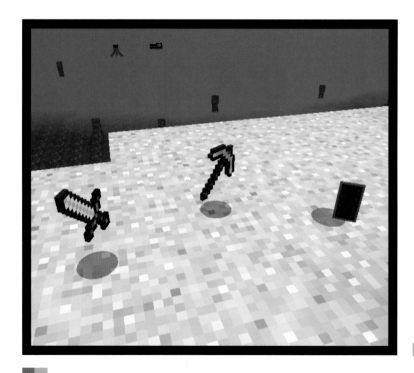

An iron sword, pickax, and shield

Diamond ore is one of the rarest and most valuable types of ore in *Minecraft*.

Experienced players use all sorts of techniques to mine for diamonds. Some dig in specific areas they think are likely to have diamond, and some make tunnels in grid patterns to help them search an area. Some enchant their equipment to make it more powerful. You can find advice from experienced players in **tutorials**. Then you can try out this advice or explore in your own way to see what works best for you.

Farming gets more interesting when you take on new challenges. You can get creative by using **mods** to add content to the game. For example, the Extended Farming mod adds new crops, such as beans and beets, and a new watering system with hoses and sprinklers.

This unusual *Minecraft* crop was created with a mod.

A *Minecraft* automated farming system

Another way to get creative is by automating your farm. You can use redstone, which is like electricity, and sticky **pistons**, which can push and pull movable blocks, to create automatic systems. These systems will water and harvest your crops and feed your animals. Then you'll have less farmwork to do and more time to mine, build, and explore. But the real fun is in building your own automated system.

STEMCRAFT

Automation in *Minecraft* reflects what happens on farms in real life. Farmers use technology to care for their crops and livestock. Sensors placed in soil check for moisture so farmers know when to water crops, and robots harvest crops. Special collars record information about livestock health and safety. For example, some sheep wear collars that send information to farmers by text. If the sheep's heart rate increases, the farmer knows the sheep may be in danger.

Just like in *Minecraft*, farmers use machinery and equipment to create better crops.

CHAPTER 4

COMING SOON

AS ANY *MINECRAFT* PLAYER CAN TELL YOU, THIS GAME ISN'T ABOUT WINNING. It's about creating a world that's always growing, changing, and getting more interesting. In fact, the entire *Minecraft* **brand** focuses on that idea.

CODECRAFT

Many *Minecraft* players use mods to change their game by adding features created by others. Mods can add content to empty areas, help players build structures and cities instantly, and even add dinosaurs to the game.

Some players create their own new features. One nine-year-old built his own teleporter.

This spacecraft was created using the Galacticraft mod.

It allows him to travel quickly from one location to another in the game. To add the features you want, you need to write code, or a set of instructions written in a programming language that computers understand. In *Minecraft*, this is modding.

Minecraft's LearntoMod software teaches players how to use two common programming languages, Blockly and Javascript, to create mods. When you write in these languages, you use combinations of words and symbols to communicate your creative ideas to your computer.

For example, a 2018 *Minecraft* update, known as
Update Aquatic, added new features to the game.
Players found new sea creatures, searchable shipwrecks,
and even a new weapon, the trident. Updates aren't
just for gameplay. The real-life MineCon, the brand's
annual *Minecraft* celebration, went digital in 2017. The
change made it possible for gamers all around the world
to connect with their favorite game. They heard from
celebrity players and got tips for better play without
even leaving home.

Minecraft's Update Aquatic provides a huge underwater world with
plenty of places to explore.

Many gaming events and promotions bring together fans of *Minecraft*.

Players will have another chance to connect in real life in 2019, when the *Minecraft* movie is released. The movie's creators haven't said much about the story line or whether mining and farming will play a large role in the movie. But it's easy to imagine a *Minecraft* character on the big screen mining for ore to craft weapons and farming to grow crops for food.

After all, *Minecraft* is a world where characters have to work to survive. And players are willing to fight for the good of their characters. The more creative you are, the more you can see that anything is possible in *Minecraft*.

With hard work and determination, you can build an impressive *Minecraft* world like this one!

GLOSSARY

brand: a group of products made by a particular company with a particular name

crops: plants grown by farmers

inventory: resources such as building materials and tools that a character carries

livestock: farm animals kept, raised, and used by people

mobs: creatures in *Minecraft*. Some mobs, known as hostile mobs, attack players.

mods: changes to *Minecraft* that players can create or add

ores: rocks from which valuable substances can be taken

pistons: parts of an engine that move up and down inside a tube and cause other parts of the engine to move

ravines: deep, narrow valleys

smelt: to obtain resources by cooking, melting, or burning a substance in *Minecraft*

tutorials: programs or videos that teach someone how to do something

FURTHER INFORMATION

Guthals, Sarah. Minecraft *Modding for Kids for Dummies.* Hoboken, NJ: John Wiley & Sons, 2015.

Learn Computer Science
https://code.org/student

Minecraft Official Site
https://minecraft.net/en-us/

Minecraft 101: Mining
http://www.minecraft101.net/g/mining.html

Minecraftopia: Farming
http://www.minecraftopia.com/minecraft_farming

Mojang Ab. Minecraft *Guide to Farming.* New York: Del Rey, 2018.

Schwartz, Heather E. *The World of* Minecraft. Minneapolis: Lerner Publications, 2018.

Zeiger, James. Minecraft: *Mining and Farming.* Ann Arbor, MI: Cherry Lake, 2016.

INDEX

PHOTO ACKNOWLEDGMENTS

Image credits:

Various screenshots by Heather Schwartz; Juan Jose Napuri/
Getty Images, p. 16; Ariel Skelley/DigitalVision/Getty Images,
p. 24; Chesnot/Getty Images, p. 28. Design element: COLCU/
Shutterstock.com.

Cover image: SkyeWeste/Pixabay CC0.